A CONTINENT OF CREATURES

The Animals of
ASIA

Nicole K. Orr

PURPLE TOAD
PUBLISHING

The Himalaya Mountains are in India. India is a country in Asia.

Welcome to Asia! Of the world's seven continents, Asia is the largest. Asia is known for its cities, and for its large areas of wilderness.

Asia is bordered by three oceans: the Arctic, Pacific, and Indian oceans. It is divided into six regions. Each of these regions has its own biomes and its own animals.

An elk stands very still. He hopes the tiger will not see him.

The Siberian (sy-BEER-ee-in) tiger is the largest cat in the world. It hunts very large prey, including elk, deer, and bears. Despite its name, it does not live in Siberia. Instead, it lives mainly in the birch forests of Russia.

A group of elephants is called a "clan."

Elephants' trunks are not just for eating grass, herbs, and bark. Their trunks can also suck up water, then shoot it up into the air so the elephants can have a shower. Elephants use their trunks to pull down tree limbs to reach fruit.

Pandas love climbing into trees and sleeping.

China's giant pandas might seem lazy. No matter how much they eat, they are always low on energy. Pandas eat mostly bamboo, but they sometimes eat meat.

Tarsiers can turn their heads all the way around to look behind them. This helps them hunt for food.

The tarsier (**TAR-see-er**) lives in the treetops of Southeast Asia. Its large eyes and ears help it hunt at night. Grasshoppers, beetles, and lizards beware — these small mammals can leap 20 feet in one jump.

The bearded vulture is an odd bird. Sometimes called the "bone eater," this bird eats almost only bones. It flies up to high cliff edges. From there, it drops the bones. The bird does this over and over until the bones have broken into small enough pieces to eat.

The brown prinia is native to Southeast Asia. They especially enjoy the dry forests of Indonesia. They build nests up to two feet off the ground.

The red-crowned crane has a red patch on the top of its head. The patch is bare skin. Cranes eat fish, rodents, grasses, berries, and insects.

Asian giant hornets have two sets of eyes.

The Asian giant hornet can eat more than 40 bees a minute. Giant hornet scouts will release a scent when they find a beehive. The scent calls other hornets to the feast.

The bees have a defense against these intruders. They will swarm the scout hornet and wiggle very fast. They will create enough heat to bake the scout hornet. The bees stay safe.

A fattail scorpion and a Chinese red-headed centipede

In warm, dry areas of the Middle East lives the fattail scorpion. It is sometimes called the man-killer because of deadly venom in its sting.

The Chinese red-headed centipede is about eight inches long. If a person is bitten, the pain can last for days. Amazingly, people have found safe ways to eat these leggy insects!

West Asian deserts provide the perfect home for the Uromastyx (yur-oh-MAS-tiks). This reptile is also called a spiny-tailed lizard. Its favorite thing to do is sleep in the sun. When it needs to cool off, it crawls into the shade of rocks.

A group of lizard eggs is called a "clutch."

Vipers keep warm by lying in the sun.

Russell's vipers slither through the grassy plains of South Asia. They often appear lazy, but their bite can be fatal. They eat small creatures, from rodents and lizards to crabs and scorpions. If hungry enough, they will even eat their own kind.

The Komodo (ka-MOH-doh) dragon lives in Southeast Asia. When it is time to take a mate, two male Komodo dragons battle for a chosen female. Using their tails to keep their balance, they stand up on their hind legs and use their front legs to fight. The loser is the one that runs away or lies down. These dragons hunt water buffalo and wild pigs.

The Komodo dragon builds
fake nests to fool predators.

Lionfish babies are called "fry."

Lionfish are the zebras of the ocean. This is because of their brightly colored stripes. The back of a lionfish is covered in spikes. Venom is stored inside each spike. The mouth of this fish is large enough to swallow smaller fish in one bite.

Vampire crabs are about half the length of your thumb.

Indonesia (in-doh-NEE-sha) is home to the vampire crab. With a dark blue-purple body, this crab looks like a creature of the night. Using its glowing yellow-green eyes, the vampire crab hunts during twilight!

The orangutan (oh-RANG-oo-tan) is the only ape with orange and reddish-brown hair.

Asia is a large place indeed. It is packed with more people and animals than any other continent in the world. So far, they all seem happy to share!

The red panda from the mountains of Nepal is just a bit bigger than an adult cat.

FURTHER READING

Books

Allgor, Marie. *Endangered Animals of Asia. (Save Earth's Animals!)* New York: Powerkids Press, 2011.

Kurkov, Lisa. *Astounding! Asian Animals.* Richmond, Victoria, Australia: Spectrum Publications, 2014.

Murray, Julie. *Komodo Dragons (Asian Animals).* Edina, MN: Big Buddy Books, 2013.

Spilsbury, Richard, and Louise Spilsbury. *Animals in Danger in Asia.* Portsmouth, NH: Heinemann Publishing, 2013.

Wang, Andrea. *Learning About Asia. (Do You Know the Continents?)* Minneapolis, MN: Lerner Classroom Publications, 2015.

Websites to Explore

Asia for Kids
   http://www.afk.com/

Asia Kids Society
   http://kids.asiasociety.org/

Ducksters: Asia
   http://www.ducksters.com/geography/asia.php

biome (BY-ohm)—Any major region that has a specific climate and supports specific animals and plants.

continent (KON-tih-nunt)—One of the seven great pieces of land on Earth.

population (pop-yuh-LAY-shun)—All of the people in one area, such as a town or country.

prey (PRAY)—An animal that is hunted for food.

wilderness (WIL-der-nis)—An area that has not been disturbed by people.

venom (VEH-num)—Poison produced by an animal.

INDEX

Printing   1   2   3   4   5   6   7   8   9

The Animals of Africa
The Animals of Antarctica
The Animals of Asia
The Animals of Australia
The Animals of Europe
The Animals of North America
The Animals of South America

ABOUT THE AUTHOR: Nicole Orr has been writing for as long as she's known how to hold a pen. She's the author of three other titles by Purple Toad Publishing and has won National Novel Writing Month nine times. Orr lives in Portland, Oregon, and camps under the stars whenever she can. When she isn't writing, she's traveling the world or taking road trips. When she was traveling in Indonesia, Orr had her water bottle stolen by monkeys. She was smart enough not to try to get it back.

Publisher's Cataloging-in-Publication Data
Orr, Nicole K.
   Asia / written by Nicole K. Orr.
      p. cm.
Includes bibliographic references, glossary, and index.
ISBN 9781624692666
1. Animals—Asia—Juvenile literature. I. Series: A continent of creatures.
   QL300 2017
   591.95

eBook ISBN: 9781624692673

Library of Congress Control Number: 2016937183

PURPLE TOAD
PUBLISHING